I Said Yes

I Said Yes

Poems and Reflections of One Girl's Journey

JOANNA DAVIDSON SMITH

Foreword by Scott Holland

RESOURCE *Publications* · Eugene, Oregon

I SAID YES
Poems and Reflections of One Girl's Journey

Resource Publications
An Imprint of Wipf and Stock Publishers
199 W. 8th Ave., Suite 3
Eugene, OR 97401

www.wipfandstock.com

PAPERBACK ISBN: 978-1-5326-6471-7
HARDCOVER ISBN: 978-1-5326-6472-4
EBOOK ISBN: 978-1-5326-6473-1

Manufactured in the U.S.A.   NOVEMBER 8, 2018

To Zach and Zadie
You changed me for the better and I am forever grateful
I love you always
Mom

To you, the reader, by picking up this book you have chosen to enter into my consciousness, our lives are forever entwined
Thank you for being you.

"I am a part of all that I have met."
—Alfred Lord Tennyson

Contents

Foreword

IF GOD IS INDEED the World's Poet, then our lives are the poetry of God. This assertion from the emerging and evolving field of Theopoetics offers a welcome alternative to creedal, propositional and systematic styles of naming ourselves and rendering God's name in history.

Joanna Davidson Smith is a theopoet who joyfully says "YES!" to the Divine and in so doing poetically names herself and all around her in this sensuous living world. Her poetry and literate spiritual reflections demonstrate that grace has not come to destroy nature but instead to more artfully reveal and expand its wonders through the writer's vision and voice.

As this writer offers a poetic account of her own life journey, we see how good writing tells a story in order to find yet another story and pens a poem to invite more poetry. Smith's writing is personal yet touches something more public or universal in the reader's spiritual and social consciousness. Writing soulfully from the microcosm of her beloved Kansas landscapes, her art allows the macrocosmic horizons of soul, body, earth, wind, fire and spirit to open before us. This poet not only puts us in touch with the awesome mysteries and metaphors of the Divine; she opens us to our own sacred and elemental passions.

As a theologian and theopoet, I find especially satisfying Smith's intersectional naming of the "universal life-source-energy/god/spirit/ presence/christ-consciousness (however you name it)" as it has guided her life and work. The sacred texts of the Judeo-Christian traditions name Spirit as *ruach* in the Hebrew and *pneuma* in the Greek. This wonderfully intersectional word means spirit, wind and breath once and at the same time.

Smith's *I Said Yes* allows us to inhale deeply and exhale freely. Breathing in we enter interior, solitary spaces of wounds, healings, light and life. Exhaling with the pleasures of the text on our breath we release memories, imaginations, hopes and dreams for our lives and the lives of all creation and creatures around us. Theopoet Joanna Davidson Smith instructs us in the magic and mystery of catching the Wind.

SCOTT HOLLAND is the Slabaugh Professor of Theology & Culture and the director of the Certificate in Theopoetics at Bethany Theological Seminary in Richmond, Indiana

Introduction

Microcosm
[mahy-kruh-koz-uh m]

Noun

1. a little world; a world in miniature (opposed to macrocosm).

2. anything that is regarded as a world in miniature.

3. human beings, humanity, society, or the like, viewed as an epitome or miniature of the world or universe.

Noun

1. a community, place, or situation regarded as encapsulating in miniature the characteristic qualities or features of something much larger

2. humankind regarded as the epitome of the universe.

THIS SHORT BOOK IS a microcosm into my soul, my life, my journey; which is in turn a glimpse into the universal macrocosm.

We all suffer, we all experience joy, pleasure, and pain. There are universal emotions and stories that resonate within each of us and each one of us, in turn, represents the universal reality. We are all connected, and we are all on a journey to discover this connectedness. As with all of us, my journey has taken many twists and turns, leading me deeper and deeper into who I am. An uncovering, re-learning and rediscovering of my true self and of universal life-source-energy/god/spirit/presence/christ-consciousness (however you name it), that has guided, shaped and never abandoned me. Throughout this book are poems and reflections I have written over the span of 30+ years. Dispersed between these are small quotes—inspirations— one-liners, that have come to me at various times throughout my journey. Sometimes these are my own thoughts; at other times they are words that have been spoken into me by something outside myself.

May you resonate with the words within, and may you also re-discover who you are, and what your soul is longing to share with the world.

The world needs your authentic voice now, more than ever.

The Beginning

THE BEST PLACE TO start is to introduce you to the sacred space in which I first discovered God (or whatever you call, or don't call, the great spiritual energy that infuses all things). This space was a farm of just over 250 acres in east central Kansas. Plenty of wildness to explore for a young girl just learning how to be in her world. The trees, grasses, cliffs, gently sloping hills, and wildlife of this spacious land have imprinted themselves upon my heart and soul. I am forever changed because of them.

The "Womb of my Becoming"; the Umbrella KD Ranch in Mont Ida, Kansas

At around thirteen or fourteen years of age I started writing "poetry"; my thoughts, feelings, longings, and dreams.
I'm not sure where that desire rose from, to write.
I don't think I'm very good at it, but it was a way for an adolescent girl, the middle of five siblings, to find her own creative voice.

There is a formula for self-reflection—three things needed to create the space to go within, to listen and to experience the spiritual presence that is the basis for all creation.

Silence + Solitude + Nature = The Contemplative Life

"In every walk in nature, one receives far more than he seeks."

~JOHN MUIR

"In your silence, when there are no words, no language, nobody else is present, you are getting in tune with existence."

~OSHO

"How important is a constant intercourse with nature and the contemplation of natural phenomena to the preservation of moral and intellectual health."

~HENRY DAVID THOREAU

"The initial step for a soul to come to knowledge of the Creator is contemplation of nature."

~IRENAEUS

I was blessed to be surrounded by this contemplative way of life, and it has taught me more than I may ever know.

The first poems you will read are ones that I wrote at an early age, at a time of self-discovery and claiming of my own voice, albeit a somewhat naïve voice.

As we progress through the pages you will also discover my own souls' progression though pain, trauma, joy, and sorrow—my journey.

Father Richard Rohr would call this my "first container," where I found order and safety.

It is also what I call the "womb of my becoming"; the space where I dwelt with God—with the spirit that flows through, and is the foundation of, all created things.

I have always been very aware of this presence in my life and am grateful.

Later, as is the typical progression of humankind, we will find what Rohr calls "disorder." This is the second container where the structure of our first container falls apart through the trials of life. This is a time of questioning, of losing hold of old power structures. A time of seeking, of going deeper into who one is as an individual. It is also a time of loss, a time that may feel like one is falling into an abyss; into a darkness or instability of unknowing. This is necessary for growth, yet it can be painful; a learning curve leading us to our highest good.

Finally, we come to what Rohr calls the third container, "reorder."

If you reach reorder, then you have come full circle back into original innocence without the naiveté. Some call this the second naiveté—where one returns to simplicity, humbleness, compassion, innocence, and a new-found sense of freedom and openness through experiential learning and wisdom.

This is where one has learned how to hold space for all that has come before—all the paradoxes of life, where everything belongs and is included.

In this space a person can look back over their life and honestly say, *"it has all led me here and I am grateful."*

This is the space from which our greatest mystical writings have emerged.

The only way we ever truly go deep into life is to fail.
To fall, and in our falling discover who we truly are . . . beautiful, broken
and beloved.

This is just a glimpse—a window—into one woman's 30-year journey from adolescent innocence to second naiveté; a microcosm of my life thus far.

You are invited to read, contemplate, and join hands with me as we take this journey together.

All are welcome.

Poetry is a "literary work." Literary is "association with the word." If we are
the poetry of God, then we are literally the word(s) of God. Jesus was the
Word.
We are as Jesus.
We are God-breathed into existence.
Words tell stories. We are God's story.
What story does your life tell?

The Late 1980s

LOVE

(1987)

Love is an object of promise . . . an ever enduring life.
Something that lasts forever.

If love were gone . . . we would be gone.
Lost forever, never to see the light.

With love, we can find our way.
Love is truth.
Truth is a promise . . . unbroken.

Love can open the door.
Love is a lantern . . . showing the Way.

With love you can't lose track
Love is the Light.

THE ROSE

(1987)

So tender and fragile, yet so full of life
A strength beyond compare
A symbol of love and courage
Should not all humankind symbolize this?
Tender and fragile, strong and enduring
Some do
Most do not
It is needed
What is wrong?
Maybe the people who have this should share it
It is the only way
One small, simple flower is stronger than most humankind . . .
What is the reason?

FRIENDS

(1987)

Do not cry
I will wipe the tears away.
Do not be afraid
I am beside you.
Do not waiver
I will hold you.
Do not be upset
I will care for you.
Remember our promise?
We are friends
Friends care for each other
I care for you.

A person is always looking—yet, rarely sees

THE MAN ON THE MOON

(1987)

Is there such a thing as a man on the moon?
Can he see us?
Does he watch us quarrel
and shake his head in pity?
Does he see us starving
and stare in wonder?
Does he see us kill
and weep?
Can he see us at all
through the dirt and grime?
If there is a man on the moon,
he is smarter than any man on earth
For he sees and knows what is happening,
and he knows how it will all end.
If there is a man on the moon . . .
I pity him
For his eyes are opened.

A DIFFERENT WORLD

(1987)

What if the world were different
What if there were no sorrow or anguish
What if there were no wars . . . no death
Would this not be wonderful?!
But wait!
There is such a world
One of joy, love and peace
One day I will go there, but I will not be alone
For my Father will be there also

In reading some of these early poems, it is amazing to see the passion and depth that already exists in such a young person—the belief system that is already established.

This "first container" of life that helped me to feel safe to be who I was at the time.

Remember this, as you look around at the young persons occupying your own lives.

KANSAS

(1988)

A place to run wild and free
An open land filled with mystery
Once there were native tribes
roaming the cliffs . . . the hills . . . the plains
The sun always at their backs
They loved this land for its free-ness
I love it for the same reason
I want to keep it this way forever
Don't let humankind destroy it
Think of the Ancient people . . .
riding across its vastness
It is a beautiful land
but will it always be this way
It is already dying out
what can we do
I want to be gone before it is destroyed
I love this land
it is beautiful

MYSTERY

(1988)

Is God real?
Where is He?
When did He come?
When will He leave?
Is He always here . . . even within our own bodies?
Why is He here?
Does He really love us?
I believe in Him . . .
but how can I?
I can't see . . . hear . . . or feel Him
Yet . . .
I know.
I know He is real
I know He loves me
and I know . . . I love Him

Fifteen years old, wondering about this mystery that she called "God."

Showing a deep faith in the unknown; still feeling safe to ask the questions.

How is humankind creating safe space, in the present time, for questions to emerge?

CAREFREE SPIRITS

(1988)

Why must we worry?
Why must we have problems and pain?
Everyone should be carefree and happy
like spirits
Let life take its course
float along with it
Let IT show you the way
Don't be disappointed
Don't let things bother you
Go on with life and enjoy it!
You only get to make one impression in life
Make it good!

Carefree Spirits was written with my best friend in mind. It seems that at this point in my life, trials were beginning to arise. The tension between the safety and beauty I had always known was rubbing up against discord, trial and sorrow. This poem has great intention, without the depths yet, of the second naiveté.

Idealistic and innocent.

LIFE & DEATH

(Oct. 1988)

Why is life so fragile?
Why can't we all be strong and enduring?
Why must we die?
Can't we all be one
a single bond of love, able to endure so much
Yet . . . we are gone
like those before us
like those behind us
We will all be gone
Are you ready to stand in front of the face of death?

Notice I marked the month of this poem. A school mate of mine had just recently been killed in a tragic car accident. This is a glimpse into the grief of a fifteen-year-old girl, wondering aloud what it all means. The paradox of life and death, darkness and light taking some form in her heart, mind and cellular memory.

The following poem is, again, a young girls idealistic dreams of love, of her relationship with a mysterious yet ever-present divine entity she calls "God." At this point she is stable and confident in what and who she believes in, prior to "disorder."

THE POWER OF LOVE

(1989)

What do you think of when you think of the word, 'love'
Do you think of passion and desire?
does it bring to mind countless memories of faceless men or women
Does it make you feel uncomfortable and scared?
When I think of love
I think of something deeper, more powerful than all of these
Feelings that really, truly MEAN something
Love is truth, honor, glory, happiness and much more
Love is everything that you need
Love changes things
You may have many possessions and relationships
but they are worthless without love
Love isn't sex
Love isn't desire or passion
It is something much more

To love others, you must love yourself
To love yourself, you must love others
Love is real and true
God gives you love
you should give God love
you will never regret it
Ever.

REMEMBER

(1988)

Remembering the times we laughed,
the times we cried.
Watching you walk proud and unyielding . . .
your back to me, heading for the future.
That you will come back, I know
When and how, I do not
We had such fun . . . such memories
As we say farewell, you dry my tears
"soon," you say . . . "soon"
I know you must leave and I understand
but why now?
I am on my own
but I will walk strongly and will not worry
For when you come back you will remember me before
and be proud.

The previous poem was a sentiment written to my closest friend during a tumultuous time in both our lives as she is moved to another state and I am left on my own; a young, naïve girl without the confidence needed to protect herself from future trauma.

Here we hang on the edge of a precipice, but I will survive.

The 1990s

HAPPINESS

(1991)

Everyone wants to have me.
People spend their lives looking for me
Sometimes, I am easy to be found
many times I am hiding
People wonder if they need me,
or if they have me already
Some think they do—all they really have is the enemy.
Don't live in pain and anger
don't live in self-mortification
If you live without me, you live in death itself
Live for life
Live for me
If you are like me, then you will have me
Smile
Have self-worth
Think of paradise, and you think of me
Humankind has many substitutes for me
None work.
You need me
everyone needs me
Goodness thrives on me.
My breath fills everything that is right,
everything that is pure
Do you not wonder who I am?
You should know
everyone should know

I wish I could introduce myself to you
I cannot

You need to find me
if you don't, then please forgive me.
The stars and constellations have known me for time eternal
Look at nature and you will see my face—my beauty—my love
Seek and you will find . . .
Is this not what is said?
Listen to your heart
Always listen to your inner self
your inner being
This is the real you

I am everywhere
I am nowhere

If you find me, introduce me to everyone whom you meet
You will not regret it
Trust me
I long to know you.

Sometimes you need to stop looking in order to find

REFLECTIONS

May, 1991

Looking into a mirror
I see a stranger staring back
One person that represents so many others,
cannot even represent herself
The vacant stare . . . the glossy covering . . .
Is this really me?

Am I just a reflection of others?

Who am I?
How do I find myself?
So many people are just reflections
Reflecting what they want to be seen
Are we frightened of the REAL person inside?
Break the mirror
Destroy the reflection
Live life for yourself
Show others truth
Don't hide anymore
Looking into a mirror
I lost the stranger
A person is staring back at me
I know who it is
I see the life in her eyes

BLINDNESS

(1991)

Is everyone blind to the outside world?
Can't anybody see the hunger and the poverty?
The wretched and the mamed?
Can't anyone smell the dirt in the air
or the stench on the ground?
Can't anybody hear the wailing cries of humanity?!
Can't anybody feel the tug in their heart?
Has everyone gone deaf?!?
Is everybody so caught up in their own world
not to see reality?

There is so much helplessness, where is the help?
The sickening voice of devastation is upon us
does not anybody hear?!?
So many people have so much,
yet we think WE are in need?!?
Open your eyes
that you may see!
Spread your arms and see how much poverty there is!
Look in all directions and take in the destruction
The destruction of ourselves
the destruction we have caused,
yet so few help to build up
Am I but a small child
So weak to do so much?

I can make a difference . . .
everyone can!
Open your eyes, your ears
Hear the wails of agony crying out for you.

The young poet is now becoming a young woman. Her anguish in seeing the devastation of lives; of creation, is evident. This progression of loss of innocence entwining with an ever-growing sense of responsibility is obvious to see.

Think back on a time in your life when you experienced anguish—a sense of frustration and a feeling of not being in control.

How did you respond?

What does that feel like in your body?

What trauma are you still holding onto, and what will bring you freedom?

LOVE (PART II)

1992

Love is a blindness
leading nowhere
Only into more and more darkness
You will be surrounded and suffocated by it
It will not lead the way
it will lose you and everything along with you

A young woman, struggling to make sense of trauma happening within and without her. Now in the birthing pains of "disorder," her sense of safety is falling apart. She is grasping for anything that may give life meaning and not finding it. She feels completely and utterly alone.

It is during and through these trials when one finds an inner strength not known before.

Be careful—If you look too hard for love, you may think you've found it

MY OWN PAIN

I have caused my own pain
I cannot blame anyone for it
Now I have to live with that pain for the rest of my life
I believe in eternal love . . .
in lasting relationships,
so what of mine?
Do I stay or go?
I know I must stay . . .
I have brought this upon myself . . .
I have caused my own pain

Love is the most simple and complex feeling in the world

ONE

(Feb. 1993)

So alone
So separated
Depression sets in

What can you do
What can you say
Turmoil and confusion collide
Everything will be fine
Nothing will ever be right again
Loved ones are far away

All you want is love
All you want is happiness
Every time you grasp something good,
Something bad takes it away

So Alone
So Separated
Depression is setting in

This is just prior to my son being born. I was nineteen years old, unmarried, still in a time and place where unmarried, pregnant women were set aside—hidden away.

This societal and familial standard had its affect on my psyche.

I felt unloved, lost, and sinful—in the most conservative and demeaning sense of the word.

No person should ever be made to feel this way.

At this point in my journey I had already made many non-life-giving choices.

I had placed myself in situations where I was taken advantage of, beaten, and even date-raped.

I was struggling to make sense of the world that I had known as a young girl, running freely through the fields, as compared to the vicious world that I now found myself in.

Love, like life, is unknown

LISTEN

(1993)

Sometimes I look around me and the world sets in
Doesn't it understand?
Does it not know that there is more to life?
everyone rushes around
day in, day out
Stop and listen to the voice
That small voice telling you what to do
telling you about yourself
about others
It is never too late to stop and listen
There is so much more to do
so much more to say.

DO it . . .
SAY it . . .
Listen to that voice
Shut the world out and listen to your inner self
Listen to your heart.

This last poem, written months after my son was born—prior to my knowledge of Centering Prayer, of Father Richard Rohr, of Thomas Merton, of Thomas Keating; prior to my study of the mystics—this poem speaks of that divine inner voice.

That spark of something—never gone—always within, that was persistent in its call.

That still, small, inner voice of the true self.

This is hope.

PRAYER

(1994)

Yesterday I thought it would never happen
but I prayed
Today I see a change
So I still pray
I do not know what the future holds
I will continue to pray

A young woman with a newborn son in the first months of marriage
seeking solace,
seeing hope.

TO LOVE & TO BE LOVED

To love is such a wonderful feeling
To give and to receive
To hold . . . To touch
To sing with happiness
To admire beauty
All are so combined
So intricate . . . So entwined

Love is a thing of beauty
The joy of a child's smile
The sound of the wind
The laughter . . . The tears
they all go together
And the maker of all looks down on us and guides us
He shows us His creation and its beauty
Look each day at the things around you
And you will see
you will see the great love He has for each one of us

SURRENDER

I give my all to thee, O Lord
I give my all to thee
I give my family, my job, my friends
I give my possessions, my weaknesses, my fears
Lord . . . I give you my life

Take me Lord, and mold me
Make me into whatever You desire
Use me Lord . . . I am a servant to You
O God, you have given Your life for mine,
now I give mine in return
Your love overwhelms me
The greatness about You, awes me

You hold no prejudice over any man or being
It is amazing!
How I want to be like You
perfect in every way
I know that this request is impossible,
but I can try

Take me as Your own, O Lord
Take me and use me
Mold me into a wonderful shape between Your loving hands

I will fail You, O Lord . . .
please understand that I will fail You
I wish this could not be

but You have created me in this way . . .
in flawed humanity
I pray that in these times
You will forgive and humble me

Show me Your great power, O God
Fill me . . . bless me
Keep me . . . love me
I am in Your hands now,
Thank You

A sweet, steadfast love and trust in the divine. A deep faith that rises from a childhood submerged in the quietness and wildness of nature.

A knowing of mystery that will give birth to an ever-deepening journey into that knowing.

She is open—she is trusting—she is vulnerable.

MY MOTHER IN ME

In the mirror I see
my mother's eyes looking back at me
so kind, so caring, so true
These are the things I see in you
My mother
When I look at my child
with so much emotion inside
I wonder if this is how you felt
When you looked into my eyes
My mother
The things I say
I have heard said before
The things I do
I have seen done before
I see you
My mother
In these things that I do
In these emotions I feel
In the words that I say
I hear you
My mother
In some long past time
An echo through the years
Mother
After you are gone
Your legacy will live on
In me
In my children
In my children's children

MY SOUL

I wish I could communicate my feelings
No one can understand or comprehend me;
only God
I want to help others
I want them to understand
How can they when I, myself, am a mystery?
I am intense
I am creative
I am artistic
I close my eyes and sway to an unknown song
I feel deeply
To the innermost part of my soul
I want to communicate this part of me
nobody seems to understand
I become hurt; I am scorned
I withdraw
I hide who I am
I no longer try
I only want to feel deep, abiding love
So deep that no one else can harm me
This is such an intense emotion;
I want to share it
I want everyone to be a part;
To be whole
I know this is impossible
We have been created differently
They cannot feel what I feel
Or understand what I understand

What can I do with this

With this deep knowing;
This intense feeling?
I feel that this is my one true gift
What can I do with it?
I want to listen
I want to feel deeply of the needs of others
To look into their eyes and see into their soul
Their heart
I want to help
Everything is interconnected
Everything has a purpose
Everyone has the power within
Open your hearts
Your minds
Your bodies
Move to the music within your soul
Meditate on your purpose;
Your very being
Find out who you are
Find out and listen
Listen

The more one learns the less one understands

Memories are God's pictures of life

COUNTRY IN SUMMERTIME

The scent of freshly mown hay
The feel of the scorching sun on an already sunburnt face
A slight rustling of the trees
Tan, lean backs; bending, working
Sweat glistening on a brow
Calloused hands
Walking down a gravel road
Warm dust sifting up between toes
The sound of a lone cow out to pasture
The distant sound of a tractor
Space is all around
Sense freedom
Sense God.
Someone is singing a distant hymn
Freshly washed laundry,
Gently swaying in a light breeze
warmed by the sun.
A dog lying in the shade
The monotonous humming of bees
Mixed scents; baking bread, sweat, grass, hay
A slithering snake; out of sight
The feel of cool grass on hot, dirty feet
Lie down and breathe in the warm, aroma-filled air
Close your eyes and feel the warmth of the sun
on a tired face
The cooling breeze caressing your forehead
Time is etched into the land, into the lines on your face;
Wisdom beyond years

Life is good
Life is beautiful.
So many smells
sounds
sights
Listening and absorbing
There are places to explore
It all holds such mystery.
This is the country in summertime
Lazy, hot, resting
This is home

TRIBUTE TO MY FATHER

My father's hands
Worn
Calloused
Gentle
Loving
Caring
Serving
His hands, his persona
My father
What can I say
Always loving
Always joking
The embodiment of every good and kind thing

My father
Always last
Always the servant
Always giving
Always sacrificing
My father
Always working
Always pushing the limits of humankind
Did God create a more perfect human?
My father
Warm
Loving
Ornery

What a love
What a light!
Look at that mischievous twinkle in his eye
Feel that gentle, down-to-earth love
Such openness
Such honesty
Has he ever experienced sorrow, pain?
He understands
He loves
He mourns
He is fully alive!
God seems to have blessed him with more life and love
Than anyone created
My father's hands
Reaching out
Loving
Warm
Calloused

CHOICES

To each their own, but down it came;
The Spirit of everlasting reign
And landed upon the seaside sand
To stop and listen to the land
What did it say? What did it do?
The warmth of life from me to you
The Spirit breathes and thrives and lives
It rides on currents of wind and sea
Then it comes to rest on you and me
The Spirit is not human, it is not beast
It only comes to you for feast
To feast it will upon your soul
And leave an everlasting hole
A place of emptiness and gloom;
A place of deep despair, but for whom?
For you
For me
For everyone my friend
So stop and listen to the wind;
For it follows the current of a distant land
and carries the wisdom of newborn sand.

PATHS OF THE HEART

The warmth of love, the happiness of life;
Combined together to form one being
A soul descended from on high,
Given so freely
Likened unto a bird-
Gently gliding on warm currents of a fresh wind.
One so complete, so lovingly made
Not even this being can understand the complications of itself
Not until it has searched for truth
And the deepest wisdom from above
This wisdom takes many years, many paths, many journeys;
All intertwined to form and create the greatest journey ever made.
Each being has a different beat
And each has its own journey
Travel your pathways and see where they can lead
They will lead to deep wisdom
To truth
This then will be made known to each
and we shall all be one.

All the previous poems-undated-were written between 1994–1996, the early years of my marriage

COMFORT ZONE

I long to be in a comfort zone
A place so warm, so loving
Where I am completely and utterly safe
Totally secure
Where no one can hurt me
I want to lock myself away from the rest of the world
To live privately
In serene warmth
Where I can lay down, feeling only peace
Where only God's love can reach me
Wrapping itself around me
I want to feel safe
I want to feel secure

Written after my husband's first marital betrayal

Do what the moment offers you—you never know how long the moment will last or if it will ever come again

FINDING COMFORT

Lord Jesus
I have learned what it is to find peace
In your bosom you hold me close
Safe and secure
I know what it is to find rest
Completely, quietly
I know what it is to surrender
In your arms
I am but a child
You hold me close
I find comfort
As I weep, you wipe the tears away
And slowly—
As you cradle and rock me—
I find rest
Deep, comforting sleep envelopes me
The warmth of your arms around me
Reassures me
I fall asleep listening to your voice
Your quiet, gentle and loving voice
Thank you, Lord,
for the comfort you give to me

A deep, abiding faith in the divine presence surrounding me—carrying me through many trials

The next poem is one that I didn't just feel inspired to write mentally and emotionally, but one where I physically felt it in my body.

It was a warm, summer day—I took a walk, barefoot, out into my father's pasture—down a dirt path.

It was surreal. It was transcendent—all time and space merged with me and around me.

It was a mystical—spiritual moment.

MOTHER EARTH

Today I felt the heartbeat of Mother Earth
And she was warm and alive!
All creation was swaying to her rhythm
Her warmth went through me
And filled me
For a brief moment I was complete
I was at peace
The earth moved me and heaven was there!

They were united through me and with me
And all was still.
I heard the earth moving
The whisperings of her past, present and future
She told me, and I knew without understanding

I am a part of her, she is a part of me
Heaven looked on
And three spirits were one

Everything is the earth's
Everyone can hear her rhythm
Touch her
Feel her warmth

She is vital
She is alive!
She sways, and moans, and sighs
Her whispers float by on a breeze
And stir your soul
You know—
And yet,
You know not
"Soon"
She says,
"Soon"
All moaning will cease
All spirits will join forevermore
We shall all be one
One in spirit
One in rhythm
Our hearts will beat in unity

A blur of time and memories.

A tumultuous teenage life—married young—young mother—betrayal—and then death.

My husband was killed in a car accident when I was twenty-seven.

My son was seven and a half, my daughter-a month shy of her third birthday.

Finality.

The 2000s

DEATH

(2000)

Who can explain this word to me?
Death.
It is so final
So unknown
Death.
It seems so black
So solemn
So scary
Death.
Shrouded figures in a cemetery
Cold, hard stones
Jutting up towards the heavens
Blank looks
Tears
Cold, misty—despair
Slow motion
Time-lapse
No more
Death.
Cold bodies
Hard caskets
Funeral flowers
The scent of Death
Reality to all humanity
Depression
Isolation

Insanity
Death.

A new beginning
New emotions
New senses
Death has shown me many things I never knew existed
I have walked in its wake
Its shadows have not overpowered me
Death
It is only a word.

When I lose myself, it is only then that I truly find myself

Out of the overflow of the heart, the eyes speak
Their salty words fill novels

Life happens whether you participate or not.
If you don't participate, it controls you

It is several years before I begin to really write again.

I still write during this time, but it is only for myself.

There is a difference in writing and writing only for oneself.

My life has been a continuous flow of the Divine, and I surrender to it again and again. This "presence" has saturated every part of my being. With every inbreath it flows through me—filling me. With every outbreath, I flow back out into it—in release and surrender; a sacred, rhythmic dance of life and love.

Language and religion have made it difficult to describe—
to explain to others—to you.
So, I am using the only language I know, and the belief system I was born into.

You can name it for yourself and the way in which you experience it.

I believe that this "Mystery" has been written, sung, painted, and ritualized the world over. For centuries humankind has tried to make sense of it, categorize it, name it. We have built religions around it, created dogma, rules and structures that try to contain it.

We cannot hold the ineffable, it will slip through our fingers like a sieve.

There is something about experiencing trauma—pain—death and life— ugliness and beauty—that opens your heart and soul up to a bigger, universal, life-giving presence.

If you are able to remain open.

There were moments throughout my experiences where I started to close myself off, but this "presence" wouldn't let me.

Something within—and without me—held on as if my entire existence depended on whatever "it" was—and "it" was right.

Remaining open is vulnerable.

Your scars show.

The rawness of who you are shows.

People "see" you and it is terrifying!

I don't know how or why I did it, but I said "*yes.*"

I said "yes" to the divine presence I had known ever since I was a child.
I said "yes" to the God who held me, carried me, and danced with me.
I said "yes" to the spirit who whispered in my ear and shared all my secrets.
I said "yes" to a universal life-source energy that kept me sane—kept me alive—kept me in presence even when all I wanted was to run—to hide away.

There was a time when I stood beneath the vastness of a blue, country sky—
my feet firmly planted in the warm grass—lifting and stretching my arms out and up, as far as I could—
Emulating the arms of the green ash that stood as silent witness before me.
I was shaking inside

I felt vulnerable
I felt powerful
I was scared
I was scarred
I was filled with anticipation
And I shouted "Yes!"
I am here
I am willing
I will go and do what you will have me go and do
I will be your servant
I will be your voice
I will spread beauty
And truth
I will love fiercely
I will have no regrets
And I will live fully!

Yes—at that moment was the moment of full surrender—Kenosis
And there was no going back.

I said yes, and all hell broke loose

REFLECTION ON A VISION

6/26/13

Chipped, faded paint on a blue window.
Eye of my soul.
Why do you look at me?
Hanging over me, illuminated.
Why?
Fear rushes in, rising in my chest.
My third and fourth energy chakras respond immediately with tightness,
queasiness.
Fear bursting forth—why?
I live in love. I seek love. I am love.
Where does this come from, where does it reside, why is it here?
How can I decapitate a feeling; an emotion?
Faded blue window, you taunt me.
Your dusty panes mock me—why?
You are old. You are worn. You are faded.
Where does your illumination originate?
How are you even suspended? Why have you been sent?
I ask questions with no answers.
I ponder and contemplate.
I meditate with smoke tendrils of incense swirling, floating skyward.
My energy is drained.
I have come face to face with my soul and fear was there.

"If it is love you seek, decapitate fear."
~Rumi

BE

4/23/13

Don't get busy
Don't hasten your life away
Sit
Sip wine
Ponder a friendship
Contemplate life
Meditate on nature
Nap
See with new eyes
Hear with new ears
Open your heart
Feel the petal unfold within you
Bloom
Smile
Laugh
Lay in the grass
Sift through the dirt
Study the ants
Watch a slug
Read a story
Ponder a story
Sit
Don't get busy
BE

Creating Sacred Space is just being present to the space that exists between us and being aware and open to what is already there

SPIRIT

2013

In the darkness of night
The Spirit waits to bring its light
For in your guilt, your shame and fear
The Spirit lingers and is always near
When we surrender what we think is lost
The Spirit holds, doesn't count the cost
For the Divine loves, embraces, forgives
Gives us grace and gifts to live

A new moon is rising-giving birth to new ideas, thoughts, theories. Giving new life to knowledge of old.

I say "Yes!"
"Yes" to the Divine, "Yes" to Oneness,
"Yes" to Love, "Yes" to Life.
Yes! Yes! Yes!

Once I verbalized an intentional "yes," it became clear—in every way—that I had chosen to embark on a life-long spiritual path.

I sold my home, quit my job of twenty years, went through training to become a Spiritual Director and later, a Reiki Master practitioner.

I was called a witch, was practically banished from my community, and told I was going to hell by persons I considered family.

All because I listened to God, followed my heart—chose to live differently, think differently, and step fully into who I was always meant to be.

And . . . because I was a woman.

DIVINE FEMININE

Wounded woman, strong of heart
Courage in fear
Love in doubt
Divine Feminine
Carving a path, creating life
Dark, narrow passages of struggle
Bright light of new life
Birth—death
Singing and mourning
Scarred and Sacred
Divine woman, strong and courageous
Nurturing and loving
Wounded yet creating
Holding space within her bosom

SONS OF ADAM

Sons of Adam
You have had your chance
For thousands of years your ego has grown
Countless innocents dead at your command
Their cries echoing across the vastness of time and space
Now is our time
The mothers of those slain
Rising up from the ashes
Bringing balance to the spheres

In your haste and might
You lost sight of true power
You have forgotten
That mercy triumphs judgment
Love trumps fear
We are the ones who will change the course of history
We have lost too much

We have been silenced
We have been burned
We have been drowned
We have been beaten
We have been called names
We have been raped
and it has not destroyed us

Your greed has blinded you
Your lust for control
Has made you go mad
You have grown complacent
We are here to relieve you
To soothe wounds
To inspire joy
To bring nourishment and love

There will be music playing
Feet dancing
You will find relief from your burdens
And you will join us
We will blend our energies into a confluence of beloved body

CO-CREATORS

Preparing the Way
Making straight the paths
Loving, singing, weeping, holding
Ushering in the Kingdom of Heaven
Touching, "see"-ing, breaking of bread

The Kingdom is here
In the wounded, aching now—we are present
Cherishing, praying, caressing
The Divine Body in every form
Love made complete
The Kingdom, the Body, the Now

*I have 'received my experience' in life and have interpreted it through the
lens of Divine feminine without theologized structure*

INVITATION TO COMMUNION

Come
Women of God, lineage of Christ, Come
Prophetess and Prostitute
Wounded, broken, lonely; Come
Empowered, confident, fearful—Come
Daughters of Rahab
Daughters of Tamar
Lineage of Deborah, Leah, Esther. Come.

All of us, Daughters of Eve
Scarred, scared, vulnerable—Come.
Body of Christ, Divine Feminine and Masculine
Joined together by Spirit—Come
Drink of His blood, Taste of His flesh
Our blood, *Our* flesh, One body
Come.

"What a Wonderful World" by Louis Armstrong has been my favorite song for years. To be able to vision what the world could be like. I have been struggling to try and discover what my passion truly is—what it is the Spirit is calling me to do and to be. Today on my daily walk, "What a Wonderful World" came into my mind and I thought, "but it already *is* a wonderful world." I can see the point of the song, but then I wondered, if we are always looking forward to what a wonderful world it can be then do we miss out on the beauty of the now?

I bought another bumper sticker for my car last week because I liked the saying, "Let the Beauty you love, Be what you do."

I thought it was just a nice reminder, but perhaps that is my passion, perhaps it is deeper than I first thought. Perhaps my destiny, my passion is to do exactly that—"Let the Beauty you love, Be what you do."

In my daily meditation I have been hearing Spirit whispering to me my own worth, my own strength and beauty. I have always struggled with low self-esteem, and it has been hard for me to grasp that I am beautiful, that I am the Beloved. Today's breakthrough helped me to see that I truly *am* the Beloved and my passion is to help others to see that they are also the Beloved. We don't have to wait for a futuristic time to enjoy a wonderful and beautiful world. We, all of us, are co-creators with the Divine, called to bring out and acknowledge our own beauty here and now, and to also see that beauty and worth in the other.

If what we long for is life-giving, then it is of God.

If what we do is life-giving, then it is of God.

The energy we bring into the world is the energy that can change the world, and that energy is already present if we just choose to accept it; to become aware of the infinite possibilities and to love them into being. One person can make a difference and I hope that by accepting my own personal call to be beauty and love to myself, and to the other, then those positive, life-giving vibrations will ripple out and affect everything around me.

May the beauty you love become what you do.

We are all the Beloved.
Once we see the beloved in each other, we are at peace.
Love brings peace and reconciles all things

PRAYER TO YAHWEH

Yahweh
I call upon your name
The very name that is the Creative Source of all Life
Grant me wisdom in the face of desperation
Grant me love and understanding in the face of hatred and ignorance
Grant me courage in the face of adversity
Grant me compassion in the face of woundedness
Grant me peace and justice in the face of violent injustice
Grant me life in the face of death, joy in times of sorrow
and contentment in times of need
May your name be always on my lips, in my heart
and resonating throughout my being.
~Amen

Your life force energy flows in and around me; creating an aura of rainbows emanating out from my Soul, my whole being vibrating in high attunement with you. We are One.

DIVINE FEMININE RISING

Currently I live in a mystical realm
Where the trees whisper their secrets and
The breezes caress my face with tantalizing breaths
The leaves shudder in ecstasy and the ground vibrates under my feet
This earth where I walk is a living organism;
A part of me that I have long since forgotten
I am beginning to awaken; to realize this is not a dream in my
subconscious, this is not an illusion
The earth is trembling
The Divine Feminine is rising once more
Wisdom is bursting forth with every brightly colored bloom and juicy,
delicious fruit
She is here, walking among us
A glimpse here, a glimpse there
A hint of sweet aroma, a subtle whisper
She is here, within you, within me
Chiding us, challenging us, embracing us
A sweet, faint smile crosses my lips as I feel her;
Rising, stronger and stronger
Coming forth in all radiance, wildness and beauty
We must pay attention
We must be ready, for she is calling to us
Asking us to join her
To bring forth peace,
To share wisdom,
To spread compassion
I am hers and she is mine

In the silence of interiority, I am wedded to the Divine

THE VOICE OF GOD

The voice of God is everywhere
It is in the song of the bird,
The crash of the waves,
The giggle of a child,
The smile of a friend
The Divine speaks in the ancient language
Of rustling leaves, drawn up through roots
From the basement of time
Listen for the voice of Wisdom that emanates
Out from deep within you
Take time in silence to sit with this voice,
this nudging,
This trembling from Source that is already within you;
deeply rooted to all that is or ever will be

Hear the Sacred voice of God through the tears
Of those mourning as they hold their loved ones for the last time; feeling
their skin against their own, stroking their hair-Being Love
God is here, God is present
Right here, right now
The Divine is within you-calling out;
drawing you into her bosom of safety, of comfort, of
Love and Life
Do you hear? Are you listening?
YOU are the Beloved
YOU are called
YOU are the voice of God
Speak.

I am drawn to the outdoors, to sitting beneath trees and lying in the grass.

I long for birdsong and whispers of wind. I crave the warmth of the sun.

They are a part of me, and I am a part of them. There is no separation.

Growing up the way I did, the out-of-doors was my church; a sanctuary created for all of us.

Cathedrals of azure sky, rocky slopes and prairie meadows. Even the sound of waves pounding is a rhythmic mantra to the gods.

This is how I connect.
So many of us are disconnected.
Seek your own way—your path to the divine.
Be present and connect again.

BE AS NATURE

Be like the tree; rooted deep into the Soul Wisdom of the earth
Flexible to sway and bow with the winds of change; the very breath of God
Be like the bird who sings joyously all day long
never tiring of its own unique song; its gift to the world
Be like the squirrels who, in the midst of gathering, always take time to
play
to leap, to chase—dashing to and fro like small children in a game of tag
Be like the butterfly that floats easily on the currents of life
bringing its own unique beauty to wherever it lands
Be like the weeds of the field; resilient and full of hope
returning again and again to their rightful place
Be Love
Just as the tree provides shelter, food and comfort to those in need—
do the same
You have been chosen
go and do likewise.

THE WIND

What I must do to understand the wind
Its comings and goings
The mysteries it carries
To sit silently
To listen to its whispers and roarings
To be still
and allow its softness to blow into my soul
That inward part of me
That understands
That knows

God is here
God is present

BLISS

Pure bliss
No heaviness, no thought
Complete knowing, complete peace
Perfect contentment
Sitting in the grass beneath the trees
sitting
sitting
sitting
Perfect, complete release
All is well

THE PINE

The pine stands stately
unapologetic
Regal
The finest of linens
drape her being
Her children scampering
flitting
singing
playing
upon her bosom
She holds it all
great spaciousness
for life to be lived

BREATH OF GOD

I am the breath of God
breathed into time and space
Infinite, yet mortal
Spirit and matter converged
I am action and life
born out of Divine love
Living, moving, breathing
breath to breath
I am life
Life creates

I am seen
then I am unseen
breath remains
swirling like the wind
whispering
I am the breath of God
eternal
unceasing

REFLECTION AT CAMP

Voices chattering
birds singing
proud trees, secure in who they are
mentors to us—rooted deep in Wisdom.
The sound of community
of singing
The beautiful symphony of all Creation
merging in sound and silence,
creating Life

THE ORIOLE

Spirit
sometimes you taunt me
like the oriole
It is a delightful game
between you and I
You call
I do not see you
a glimpse here
a glimpse there
both my impetus
as well as my nemesis
Challenging
Calling
I sense your presence
Playful searching
running here and there
When seen in all your splendor
I stop.
Transfixed

All of the cosmos is within me
I am light and dark
chaos and peace
struggle and contentment
I am a blessed drop of Divine consciousness
I am eternal
I am.

There are no labels—there are only people
Beautiful Divine drops of Me
They are all miracles

I was sitting in meditation one day—outside, cross-legged, facing the south hay meadow, when the words above were spoken into me.
The "Me" written here does not refer to my person, the "Me" refers to the one who spoke the words.

I am nothing, absolutely nothing; and yet, I am everything

Complete Disorder

I moved—Away from my sacred space—It was hell—
It had to be done.
Life had grown bitter for us; poison had spread like a virus throughout our community.
We were ostracized.
We were the ones who heard whispers behind hands and noticed the disapproving looks.
It was time to move on and to be free.
It was agony.
I thought it would destroy me

.

.

.

.

.

.

.

.

.

.

.

A NEW HOME

How is this fair, how is any of this fair?!
Like a fish out of water I am gasping for air
Searching and clutching at straws that aren't there
This is not my home
Why am I here?
I want to go home
I am well acquainted with sorrow
I don't know if I can get up this time
Highs and lows
Tragedies and joys
They have bound us
It is intricate
Woven—
A closeness borne out of living.
These are my people
The agony of being alone
Being apart from my community
Severed—
Broken
Heal these wounds, Oh Lord
Heal these wounds

CRY OF DESPERATION

There is no joy left, my bones are seeped;
I am dry and brittle
I am as a lifeless corpse
I no longer want to play the victim, yet who do I have?
I have never been so alone
No reputation, no community, no family, no friends
I am lost in a vast sea of despair
Hopelessness has covered me
I call out to what I know as God
I weep
And yet, nothing
Where do I go from here?
I am but a shadow; a mist
Do I even exist?!
I still feel pain, separation, loneliness;
It must be existence, but what kind?
To whom can I turn?
Who hears the cries of pain from my tortured soul?
I long for communion;
To feel the lightness of joy once again
Has this become my reality?
I never would have thought I would be on this path
It happened so suddenly, like a jolt out of nowhere
What can be the purpose?
I love but feel as if I am not loved
I have fully lived and yet no one seems to notice
I have surrendered again and again and I am exhausted
How much more must I endure?

How much longer?
Darkness is all around me, closing in
Waves of hopelessness continue to engulf me
I cry out, there is so much pain but no one hears
It is as if I no longer exist,
Like a dream where others walk by and do not see
I am here! Do you not know?!
Why has this happened . . .
Then a faint, whisper of a voice says to me,
"You asked to be like me, you have surrendered to me fully.
You bear my cross; you drink from my cup."
No, I did not ask for this! Please, make it stop.
 I am not strong enough
And the voice said, *"But I am"*
"I AM"
I. am.

*I laid myself low so that God could find me, and in the midst of my
surrender despair found me, leaving me more wretched than before. Isolated
and full of doubt, I screamed out in anger. "Why?! Why have you
abandoned me when I have given all to you? Why do you sit in the shadows
and scoff at me?"
I collapse, exhausted at the battle, and silently the Christ tenderly picks me
up.*

I have been brought low so that you might be resurrected within me

I looked for God and lost myself.
I found myself and therein lay God.

HOLDING SPACE

I lay myself low—God Incarnate—Lord Jesus—
a vessel of pure, life-giving love—Innocent—
Sweet—Vulnerable—Humble

Here I am—A vessel—A container to hold
space—Love—Compassion—Hatred—Lies—Deceit—
Safe Space—Holding—Womb-like—
Witness to all that is
The Universe in microcosm—Infinite Reality—
God in me—Me in God—Source—Creator—
We are One—Swirling—Around and Around

Where do I end—Where do you begin—
A blurring of time and space—
Everything exists because of you—
Love reaching out—Love Infinite—Holding—
Seeing—Loving

All is well

I am a vessel, a holding container, a womb that is
co-creating, still giving birth,
still creating

God is Spirit
God is Love
Those who want to commune with the Divine must do so in Spirit
Those who wish to experience God must do so through channels of love
Overwhelming love
That washes over you and through you
Creating a desire within you to spend the rest of your life
reciprocating that love

HOME

What is 'home' to you?
For me, coming home is like running ecstatically into the arms of my
lover after a separation
Where warmth and knowing can embrace my vulnerability and I am safe,
secure, surrounded and wrapped up in pure peace
What happens then, when 'home' is taken away?
How do you re-define what 'home' is?
How do I?
Where can I find 'home'?
Jesus, in the garden of Gethsemane, pouring himself out before his father
Racking with sobs
Alone
Separated
Isolated
No security, crossing over into the unknown
Drained
Exhausted
Surrendering,
Surrendering
Kenosis: Self emptying-release-surrender-letting go
"Not my will, but thine . . . "
When we don't know the answers
When we aren't on solid ground
When home is lost
When we are too tired and ragged to go on
When no one seems to understand
I fall face-down
Arms spread out wide

Surrendering
I cannot hold on anymore
I am not in control
I feel powerless

A part of me wants to die
A part of me needs to die
Kenosis: Self emptying-openness-surrender
This is where it is
In this space
You are embraced, just as you are
You are seen
You are loved
"Not my will, but thine . . . "
Beyond comprehension
Kenosis
This is home

"You are part of everything and in a sense, part of everybody . . . . the only way that I can be at home everywhere is to be sure that I am at home somewhere."

~HOWARD THURMAN

Wisdom is surrendering to what we do not know and trusting in what we do

LONGING

There is a longing deep within each of us.

A grieving for something lost that we can't quite put our finger on.

A burning desire to be 'whole' again, whatever that means.

What is it that is missing? What is broken that needs mended?

What is lost that we are seeking?

Oneness, Unity, Wholeness.

That which we were before our birth.

That which we long for until we die.

Home.

THE SEEKER

I didn't think my life would turn out this way. Who does? I'm an idealist and I think it has ruined me. I also have multiple personalities; at least, that's the way I see it. I know who I am. I met her at a young age. She's actually pretty awesome; carefree, full of life and joy, bubbling over with love, always mesmerized by the natural world.

She sings and skips and twirls.

She dances in the rain and runs through tall grasses, she's not afraid of bugs or snakes or anything for that matter. She sings at the top of her lungs and spreads her arms out wide, absorbing all that is. She lies down in the cool grass and allows the sun to soak into her body.

This is me. This is Joanna, or at least that's the name I've been given. I am really Spirit, Feminine Energy, a drop of the Divine.

I am the deliciousness of the world. I know this, so why the struggle? Why the multiple personality complex?

I also tend to focus on my egoic self. You know, the one that stresses and worries and wonders how the hell she's going to pay for doctor's appointments and groceries and the oil change for the car. Not to mention college for her kids, laundry detergent, a car—period. That self that cries and cries because she sees the other self, the one she knows is real and yet cannot quite get to her. So I try to be both, to do both. And it's not working.

On the one hand, I know that life is about relationship, love, good food, chocolate and all the things that bring each one of us pure, innocent, sweet joy and bliss.

On the other hand, life also brings us struggle and pain, death and heartbreak. Now my true self, the one that is carefree and dances in the rain, knows that I need both.

I need the struggle, I need the pain, I even need the death. Otherwise there is no sharpening and honing of empathy, compassion, love, deep abiding joy and resurrection, but like I said, I'm an idealist. I see how the world can be. I see and deeply feel, in my bones and soul, that life is glorious and beautiful and full of perfect peace. So here I am. Caught between my two selves and wondering how I got here, and how can I get out, or change, or grow up into that true self immortally.

I have struggled, just as we all have. I've had major disappointments and pain and heartbreak, just as we all have. I have suffered death and even resurrection and yet I am here, in the midst of failure; or at least the feeling thereof. I feel that I have truly strived to be faithful to my authentic self.

I have strived to do and be the person that Spirit has called and nudged me out to be.

I am perfectly content being a contemplative, being a healer, sharing love and spreading joy. This is all good. This feels 'right' to me. Why then the 'not having', the lack of abundance, the great financial strain?
This poverty; this literal, physical poverty must be a teacher. It must point to a greater poverty and yet I cannot put my finger on it. What am I missing? Why *this* struggle? Why *this* shame, this guilt? Why *this* poverty of Soul? I am lost. I am desperate. I am in need. Is this seeking all there is?

WINTER

Resting in the silence and solitude that this season brings.
Holding spaciousness for all creation;
birthing new life in the darkness.

THE STRUGGLE

Oft times I lie in bed at night
Warm tears streaming down my cheeks
Not knowing how to move forward
Knowing I can't go back
Doubt and fear lay waste to my Soul
Caught somewhere between society and my truth
Struggling to bridge this deep chasm
I feel hopeless and divided
Aching to step into my truth
Aching to be whole

Tethered to standards that will never free me
Dreaming, visioning my joy; my peace
Longing to let it all go
Longing to unshackle, to take the leap
To break freely into the unknown
I am in a spin cycle that has no end
Knowing fully a paradise I can never grasp
A constant struggle; one step forward, three steps back
Oft times I lie in bed at night
Warm tears streaming down my cheeks

The work happens in the silence

THE OMEGA POINT

Going down into that deep place within me
The space wherein lies my Source
Intimate, infinite, indescribable Mystery
As Teilhard states, the "Omega Point"
That within me, yet other than me
Drawing me forward
A magnetic true North
A force that I cannot be apart from
Drawing me deeper into itself
I can struggle
In which I then cause an outward struggle
Or I can fully trust and surrender
Falling into its flow
Abundance
Love
Peace
Deep joy
Pulling
Calling
Gentle and constant
I am being pulled into a new way of being
A new way of seeing

The truth of life is found in the darkness

CYCLICAL NATURE

There is a rhythm to life
Living and dying
Cyclical Nature
Never-ending
Loving
Living
Grief
Sorrow
Joy intermingled with pain
A universe contained in one spark
It falls and is buried
A miniscule "big bang"
Bringing forth life
Creating
Rhythmic
Cyclical
Unending

Life ebbs and flows all around me

If infinity and intimacy are both reality
then let us move beyond our small mind constructs
to create a more spacious, inclusive world for all.
It's time

As I linger over the aromatic warmth of my cup of cocoa I am reminded of how blessed I am. I also remind myself to do this more often; lingering, being appreciative, loving life, remembering.

In times like this I think to myself that I will not forget, that I will always be grateful, and of course that is my intention. An intention that will fail, time and time again, and yet, that is okay. I have a pretty decent life. I have also had my share of struggles; such is the process of living. Today I am thankful. I am thankful for a warm, cozy home. I am thankful for family that supports and loves me. I am thankful for two of the most beautiful children a mother could ask for. I am thankful for work and play, for health and for an ever-growing hunger to dive deeper into the wisdom of love, community, silence and laughter.

Oft times I watch the news or search my media sites and I feel a strong sense of urgency. A sense of urgency to strike out, to act, to change what I see or hear, and there may be a time and place for that. Today I know that true transformation must be in small ways, every day; a phone call here, a letter there, a hug, a smile, a plate of cookies, a listening ear, a hot cup of cocoa on a cold day.

There is a shift happening. Many of us are waking up from what can only be described as a stupor. I am no longer living in the fantastical days of my childhood and am realizing that something has been drawing me forth to this time and place for a specific purpose. I sense in many this same urgency, this same hunger for justice, a hunger for deeper connection and for a more peaceful and sustainable planet. I have known this since I was a child and yet there is something different about this knowledge today. The consciousness of humanity, of creation, has shifted in such a way that this new awareness is being ushered in. We are ready for love to transform us. In my scriptural tradition it is said to be a time of harvest.

Don't you have a saying, 'It's still four months until harvest'? I tell you, open your eyes and look at the fields! They are ripe for harvest.

~JOHN 4:35

I am ready. I am willing. I am blessed and grateful for all the "good" and the "bad." I trust that there is a greater picture and I am but a small piece.

I cannot know the how's and why's, but I can know, in the deepest part of me, that love is the answer.

I am thankful for each person in my life and the impact they have had, I am a different person for meeting them. I am just as I am intended to be and hope to live in such a way as to be a life-giving force on this earth and to each of you as well. May each of us struggle to live in love, to spread these ripples wide, and in doing so, transform our communities, our families and ultimately the world.

Where I am, you are welcome

JOURNEY HOME

We are all born of one Spirit
On differing paths
In differing spaces
We are intermingled
We are dispersed
Working our way back to one another
Individual threads in one tapestry
Seeking that which binds us
Love is the goal
Love is the answer
Love is who we are as well as who we become
Love is the Source as well as the path
Love is both joy and sorrow
Love is all
As we journey, may we become aware
As we become aware, may we continue the journey

You must guard love at all costs
For love is the source and flow of the universe
The very root of your being

REMEMBRANCE

Warm, inviting sunshine penetrating deep within my body
Selfless and unhindered ambition
Joy. Singing. Carefree.
Looking gleefully out over a vast expanse of blue sky laced with the
occasional cloud
Swaying green grasses
The chirping of birds,
the buzzing of insects only found on a warm day
So much freedom
So much joy
So much beauty
I am one with a multitude
All are connected
Innocent knowing
Pure bliss radiating out from my heart space
Running down the length of my limbs,
Tingling out to the tips of fingers and toes
Pure beams of light bursting forth from within and without
All surrendered to and surrounded by this great expanse of Love
This is 'God'
All Creation knows
When do we forget?

We are the beautiful and beloved body of the Cosmic Christ, walking around in flesh and bone. Laughing, joking, drinking, playing, drumming, dancing, making love, rejoicing, singing, mourning, hurting. Every one of us is the image of the Divine. Sheer beauty, both flesh and Spirit. Living our lives and touching those around us,
we create our world.

THE LOTUS

I am a buddha
in the center of a lotus
content
spacious
grounded
hues of rainbow
flow out from me
into my world

AWAKEN TO DIVINE SPIRIT

Let Wisdom and compassion drip off you like honey
Be willing to sit in the dark
Be the light and warmth that dissolves
Carry within you a candle; burning, burning
Spread light and joy as you go forth
Creating all-embracing space
Share sorrow with sorrow
Joy with joy
Show compassion for the downtrodden
Love for the angered
Sit with others in the dark
Do not be afraid
Hold the fragrant warmth in your hands
Spread it out behind and before you
Awaken and listen
Awaken and love
Awaken and be
You are the Divine Spirit
You are
I AM

The way Mothers Day is celebrated has bothered me for some time. I have noticed its insensitivity towards those who are unable, or who have chosen not to have children—or to those men who may be the feminine aspect of nurturance for others. I have come to believe that gender is a spectrum; whether you are born biologically male or female.

We all have feminine and masculine traits and characteristics—the following reflection is for those who find themselves leaning more toward the nurturing, empathetic end of this spectrum.

SPIRITUAL MOTHERHOOD

What is motherhood? There is a wide spectrum of people in the world; some more masculine than others and some more feminine than others. If you are on the more feminine aspect of this spectrum then you may already be considered a mother.

Biological maternity is not the only way of being a mother.

A mother is also one who has *spiritual* maternity. In other words, one who is more intrinsically nurturing, compassionate, caring, and who tends to listen and hold, bind up wounds, and love through the softness and openness of the heart.

You do not need to have given birth to be called, 'Mother'. There are hundreds of people around the world desperately seeking and in need of, a mother; someone to love them, to care for them and to listen to their problems, joys and sorrows. Being a mother is the very essence of femininity. It is so interesting that many children already grasp this understanding at a very young age, by caring for and nurturing siblings, stuffed animals, dolls and pets. They are showing us the intrinsic mothering love of God.

In a way, we are all called to be mothers, if we love as Christ loves. We open our arms wide to embrace the lost, the hurting, and the confused. We tenderly apply salve to the wounds of those crying out for help. We carry those who cannot carry themselves. We listen, and we love from the deepest womb of our soul.

God places people in your path and it is your task to love them, to care for them, to allow them the safe, loving spaces where they can be free; free to be who God has created and called them to be. Safe to learn how to be vulnerable, safe to learn how to truly listen, safe to learn how to trust. Safe to learn the art of caring for the wounds of others by learning how to care for their own.

Mothers, today is a day to celebrate all you are and all you were created to be. Whether you have your own biological children at home or far away, whether you have adopted or foster children, whether your child has passed from this earth, whether you have or will ever have biological children—You are the mothers of Creation. You are the mothers of the earth.

Spiritual children are given to you, they *will* come. Open your hearts and eyes to see these children who need you, who seek you. Be the mothering aspect of God to them; teaching them well and loving them into Being.

Relationships always come first
Your 'connectedness' to the Divine, to yourself, to others,
to the whole of creation!
Love always trumps fear.
Hospitality never involves judgment.

THE LONGING

There is a particular that drives me
That haunts my dreams
My Soul
There is a longing that draws me forward
That feeds me
And guides my steps
How do I release the particular
And embrace the longing?
(I am still held in chains by the embrace of the Divine felt at the farm)

ENCAPSULATION

I must break open
This shell of my being
Embraced by God within my smallness
I am only a seed
To be broken open
To flourish
I don't want to leave this safe, comfortable space
This warmth
Where I am understood
Where I am fully known
Fear keeps me here
Awaiting the time of wholeness
At the last breaking open

As I am breaking open—freely—of my own accord, I am re-discovering the abundant life. This life is one that embraces the whole, and allows me to be my authentic self, even in the midst of chaos and struggle. I continue to mourn the losses I have experienced, but I am aware that these losses have brought with them, openings into a deeper wisdom and knowing.

It is haunting

And at the same time, peaceful

I am grateful for all that I am, and all that I am still learning and un-learning

There is freedom in that

"Don't run away from things that are unpleasant in order to embrace things that are pleasant. Put your hands in the earth. Face the difficulties and grow new happiness."

~THICH NHAT HANH

Meditative practice—living in the present moment—focusing on the good, the lovely, the beautiful. Holding and understanding the suffering; looking deep into the root causes of it, is freedom.

The Buddha called suffering a Holy Truth; a kind of suffering that can show us all the way out—the way to freedom.

We are suffering. The United States is suffering. The world is suffering.

How do we hold this suffering and not succumb to it? I am deeply saddened. Saddened that so many in this world do not see their inherent blessedness, their belovedness. The only way to stop the cycle of violence is through love.

We must not react but respond out of love, grace and mercy.

Some will not understand, maybe one day they will—maybe not, but it is the only way. Love always will win, and grace and mercy will always triumph over judgment and hatred. By tradition I am a Christian, but that does not matter, what matters is that I am an awakened being. Somehow through my own suffering and my own experiences of God, I have discovered that I am perfect and holy and blessed just how I am—as are you.

You may not know it yet, but you are.

So was the Orlando gunman, and Hitler. So is Donald Trump and Hillary Clinton and the Koch brothers and the neighbor across the street. So is the person who cut you off in traffic, the "friend" on Facebook that you disagree with, and so were all the beautiful lives that have been cut short in predominantly minority neighborhoods, and in multiple schools around our nation.

I believe in something that is bigger than all our politics, our country and our world.

I also believe that this something is a part of each one of us—that through this something we are all held, inextricably bound to one another. In my tradition, I call it Christ Consciousness or Spirit—you may call it something else or not even believe in it.

That's okay too.

I believe that if you sit long enough in silence, gaze upon a waterfall uninterrupted, consciously walk down a gravel road, really *look* at a sunset, tenderly hold the hand of someone struggling for their last breath, look deeply into the eyes of someone you love, listen to the melodious laughter of children, or see the freedom in which a bird soars—you already know.

Something deep inside you is touched—maybe there is no explanation, but there is a deep, abiding knowing. There is something outside of you, yet also a part of you, calling your name; drawing you ever closer into a mystery that you long to be part of. Deep calls unto deep, like calls to like.

Sit and listen. Be still and know . . . Practice mindfulness; the ability to live in this very moment. What are you allowing into your thought process; your body, your mind, your soul, your very inmost being?

What have we—as a culture, a society, a country, a world—allowed into our collective conscience?

This is an important topic for discussion.

What are we taking in, what are we ingesting?

What are we creating?

In community, what can we discern together, to resist and remove from, our collective conscience?

What is it that we can envision together, to create and manifest as one consciousness?

Finally, brothers and sisters, whatever is true, whatever is noble, whatever is right, whatever is pure, whatever is lovely, whatever is admirable—If anything is excellent or praiseworthy—think about such things.

~Philippians 4:8 (NIV)

AUTUMN REST

Crisp, white curtains swaying gently in a breeze that speaks of freshly
mown hay, sunshine and birdsong.
Trees rustling outside the window, full of drying,
brightly colored leaves—
telling their story of life.
The hum of an insect contentedly flying about
its song lazily repeating in the back of my consciousness.
A setting sun that is casting autumn hues over a closing day
Another passage of time; my life.
Comforted under a handmade quilt of embroidered flowers
lying back on large cushioned pillows
Settling into a warm, soft, hazy, yet blissful rest
Knowing I will soon be free
Nostalgic, surprisingly calm, joyful.
My children are nearby
the low murmuring of grandchildren in an adjoining room
playing a game.
Such sweet endings
time is good today
Life is beautiful.
My time has come to rest
to enter into another realm
not completely unknown, yet full of mystery.
I am complete
I am joy
I am life.
The crisp, white curtains sway gently in a breeze that will carry me home

*When I am immersed in the depths of that final baptism, I will emerge from
out of the dark waters into the omniscient embrace of the Creator*

HERE I AM

Here I am
Standing in the middle of heaven and earth
One foot in a mystical realm, the other on a 3rd dimensional plane
Living here with stark reality and deep, abiding presence
Called to bridge a nonexistent gap

Living, breathing, dancing into awareness—the Mystery

Gently guiding, bending, twisting—a delicate balance between the
appearance of secular and sacred

Here I am
Listening for that still, small voice; waiting for ruah—
breath of God, to come rushing in
Bringing healing through touch, through voice,
through vision
Called to be salt and light to a world unaware
The beauty is here, just beneath the surface
Beneath the scars we have helped to create

Here I am
Pointing in a new direction
Drowning out the chatter of voices and looks that disapprove
Standing on both heaven and earth—How firm a foundation

There is no separation, it is only illusion
An illusion that builds ego and destroys truth

An illusion that brings death and destruction masquerading as good
intention and morality

Here I am
Breaking chains, tearing down false institutions
Allowing the breath of life to freshen dark corners and dingy halls
Decimating sanctuaries created by man and exposing
roots of injustice

Here I am
Leading into fresh, green pastures and sitting with you beside still waters
Waters that cleanse and refresh
Words and space that renew and open the soul
Allowing Divine Love to enter in
A balm for the wounded, a deep rest for the fatigued

Here I am
Remaining firm
Raising awareness
Being Love

A deep call reverberating up from the depths of myself
From the depths of the earth
Calling me out to be who I am
Integrating all into One
"Yes!"
Here I am

Thank you for traveling with me. I have come full circle—entering into second naiveté.

If this journey ends now—I am full, I am grateful, I am blessed. If I am given the gift to continue on, then I will move forward in anticipation, hope, and knowing that I do not know—and that is okay.

I have faced many demons and I am free—authentic to live life moment by moment, continually searching and seeing the beauty that is around me— to be the young girl who grasped how deep and wide the love of the Divine is. Living with awe, curiosity and wonder at all she encounters. Continually evolving as the Divine draws her into an ever greater awareness and greater love into a universe that is always expanding, abundant and inclusive.

This is life, and life is good

"Life is not to break us down. Life is not to hurt us. We are here to grow. We are here to learn. We are here to have an adventure."
~TANAAZ, CREATOR OF *FOREVERCONSCIOUS.COM*